*Primary Sources of the Abolitionist Movement*

# Abraham Lincoln, the Emancipation Proclamation, and the Thirteenth Amendment

B. J. Best

Cavendish Square

New York

Published in 2016 by Cavendish Square Publishing, LLC
243 5th Avenue, Suite 136, New York, NY 10016

Copyright © 2016 by Cavendish Square Publishing, LLC

First Edition

Cataloging-in-Publication Data

Best, B.J.
Abraham Lincoln, the Emancipation Proclamation, and the 13th Amendment / by B.J. Best.
p. cm. — (Primary sources of the abolitionist movement)
Includes index.
ISBN 978-1-50260-530-6 (hardcover) ISBN 978-1-50260-531-3 (ebook)
1. United States. — President (1861-1865: Lincoln). — Emancipation Proclamation —
Juvenile literature. 2. Lincoln, Abraham, — 1809-1865 — Juvenile literature.
3. Slaves — Emancipation — United States — Juvenile literature. 4. Constitutional
amendments — United States — 13th — Juvenile literature. I. Best, B. J., 1976-. II. Title.
E453.B4475 2016
973.7'14—d23

Editorial Director: David McNamara
Editor: Amy Hayes
Copy Editor: Cynthia Roby
Art Director: Jeffrey Talbot
Senior Designer: Amy Greenan
Senior Production Manager: Jennifer Ryder-Talbot
Production Editor: Renni Johnson
Photo Researcher: J8 Media

The photographs in this book are used by permission and through the courtesy of: Universal History Archive/UIG via Getty images, cover; Public domain/File:Gordon, scourged back, NPG, 1863. jpg/Wikimedia Commons, 5; Photo Researchers/Science Source/Getty Images, 6; John Parrot/ Stocktrek Images/Getty Images, 8; Library of Congress, 11, 12, 13, 14; Hulton Archive/Getty Images, 17; Library of Congress, 20, 22; Chicago History Museum/Getty Images, 23; Library of Congress, 27, 29; Everett Historical/Shutterstock.com, 33; Library of Congress, 34, 36, 37, 40, 41, 44; Public domain/Dbking/File:The 15th Amendment to US Constitution.jpg/Wikimedia Commons, 46; Library of Congress, 50, AFP/Getty Images, 52; Library of Congress, 53.

Printed in the United States of America

# CONTENTS

# Slavery in the United States

The United States was very different in 1809. The country was only twenty-two years old, and had seventeen states. There were obvious differences in technology. Citizens didn't have the Internet, television, radio, or the telegraph. They didn't have cars, electricity, or indoor plumbing. The United States was a different society, too. Most importantly, it was a society that allowed slavery.

Slaves would perform unpaid work for their owners, often for life. They were not treated as people, but property. Slavery was originally permitted in all of the United States. But some white citizens felt that owning slaves was immoral. In 1777, one year after the Declaration of Independence was signed, Vermont became the first colony to outlaw slavery.

However, many felt slaves were important to help the country grow. The colonies were growing, and relied heavily on agriculture to provide food for the population

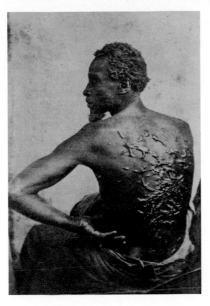

Many slaves were treated poorly and often physically abused. This slave has many scars on his back from being repeatedly whipped.

as well as **cash crops** to sell. The most common cash crop was tobacco. Since tobacco requires a lot of work to grow, farmers needed additional people to work for them. A Dutch company first brought African slaves into the United States in the early 1600s, and from that point, the slave trade grew rapidly.

By the 1800s, slavery died out in the Northern states. Agriculture became less important and the region slowly became more industrial by building mills and factories. More and more states passed laws that emancipated, or freed, the slaves.

But Southern states still relied heavily on agriculture. Eli Whitney patented the cotton gin in 1793. The cotton gin efficiently removed the seeds from the cotton to allow it to be used to make cloth. Cotton quickly became a profitable and important crop for the South. Large farms called **plantations** expanded, and required more and more slaves to harvest the cotton.

Life for slaves was very difficult. They were sold at auctions and then owned by their masters. Some masters could treat their slaves kindly, but many treated slaves as if they were animals. Slaves did exhausting work, regardless of age, with little hope of being free. They were

CREDIT SALE OF A CHOICE GANG OF 41
**SLAVES!**
COMPRISING MECHANICS, LABORERS, ETC.,
FOR THE SETTLEMENT OF A CO-PARTNERSHIP OF RAILROAD CONTRACTORS.
BY I. A. BEARD & MAY, I. A. BEARD, AUCT'R.
WILL BE SOLD AT AUCTION, AT BANKS ARCADE, MAGAZINE STREET,
ON TUESDAY, FEBRUARY 5th, 1856,
AT 12 O'CLOCK,
A VERY VALUABLE GANG OF SLAVES,

Because slaves were treated as property and not people, they were sold like other goods. This notice advertises a slave auction.

whipped or beaten. It was against the law to educate them. Slaves were regarded as subhuman.

In the early 1800s, tensions grew between the North and the South. Because slavery was unjust, some people, especially in the North, wanted to end it everywhere in the United States. These people were known as **abolitionists** because they wanted to abolish, or end, slavery. Abolitionists met opposition in the South because Southerners wanted to protect their farms and their ways of life.

This issue became heated. People began to argue each side more and more strongly. By the middle of the 1800s, slavery caused violence between those who believed in it and those who didn't. It became an issue that would tear the nation apart.

In 1809, a boy was born in a one-room log cabin in rural Kentucky. As he grew into an honest, hardworking young man, no one knew how he would change the nation—and its stance on slavery—forever.

# CHAPTER ONE

# Abraham Lincoln and His Rise in Politics

**A**braham Lincoln, the sixteenth president of the United States, is known as "The Great Emancipator." On January 1, 1863, he issued the **Emancipation** Proclamation, which began the process of officially ending slavery throughout the United States. Both historians and the general public frequently identify him as one of the greatest presidents our country has ever had. However, you might be surprised to learn this great president had very simple beginnings, and that his beliefs about slavery developed throughout his life.

Lincoln was born on February 12, 1809, in a log cabin in central Kentucky. At the time, Kentucky was one of

This painting shows an idealistic, heroic version of a young Lincoln. He is portrayed as a hardworking log splitter.

the most western states in the United States. The Lincolns lived a frontier life of farming. His father had initially been wealthy but lost his land in court cases due to incorrect ownership papers. Having lost their land, the Lincolns continued to move west as the country grew. They moved to Indiana when Lincoln was seven years old, but his mother died when he was nine. His father remarried, and the family moved again when Lincoln was twenty-one. They settled outside of Decatur, Illinois, and Lincoln is most strongly associated with that state.

## Lincoln's Early Politics

Lincoln first entered politics when he ran for the Illinois state legislature in 1832, but lost. In 1834, Lincoln ran for the state legislature again and won a seat in the Illinois House of Representatives, where he served until 1840. Lincoln was a member of the Whig political party. The Whigs opposed both slavery and abolition. They believed slavery was unjust, but it could not be legally abolished in states that allowed slavery. They hoped to abolish it in future territories as the country expanded westward, and that it would eventually die out on its own. Lincoln was then elected to the US House of Representatives in 1846.

Abraham Lincoln, the Emancipation Proclamation, and the Thirteenth Amendment

# A Frontier Education

When Lincoln was a boy, some people considered him lazy. Yet, as he grew up, he became more responsible. He assisted with household chores. He was particularly good at using an axe to make split-rail fences—a trait for which he would later become famous. He had very little formal schooling. He attended school a month here, a few weeks there. He said his total time in a classroom "did not amount to one year." However, Lincoln loved to read. He gained the education he didn't receive in the classroom by reading books by writers such as Benjamin Franklin and William Shakespeare, newspapers, and the Bible.

Even when he was a young man, Lincoln had a gift for speaking and language. His neighbors knew him as intelligent and witty. Lincoln loved to tell stories and jokes. He held jobs as a farmhand, postmaster, and surveyor. He became known as a dependable and honest person—and from these experiences people gave him the nickname "Honest Abe." Eventually, Lincoln studied very hard and became a lawyer. He was praised as being logical and well spoken.

He pledged to serve only one term, accomplished little, and afterwards returned to his law practice in Illinois.

In the 1850s in the United States, the issue of slavery grew larger. Increasing numbers of people, especially in the Northern states, felt slavery was cruel and immoral. The split between the Northern and Southern states was partially due to the economies of each. In the North, industrialization was growing. Companies in the North used factories to produce large amounts of goods. People in the North felt workers should be equal—all people have the same rights to be paid for their work. The economy in the South was based more on agriculture. The South had large plantations that grew crops like cotton or tobacco. The owners of these plantations needed workers to plow, plant, harvest, and perform many other farm tasks. These owners bought slaves. If they lost their slaves, they worried that they would also lose their ability to earn money.

## Stephen Douglas and the Kansas-Nebraska Act

In 1854, another man from Illinois caused Lincoln to become active in politics again. He was Stephen Douglas. Lincoln became friends—and rivals—with Douglas back when Lincoln was a state representative in Springfield, the capital of Illinois. Since that time, Douglas had become an influential and powerful politician. He was an associate justice of the Illinois Supreme Court, a US representative, a US senator, and a presidential candidate.

As a senator, Douglas helped write and pass the Kansas-Nebraska Act of 1854. As the United States established more territories, which could become states, people asked if those territories would allow slavery. Earlier, in 1820, the US Congress agreed to the Missouri Compromise. This law said new territories north of the southern border of Missouri could not allow slavery. The Kansas-Nebraska Act created the Kansas and Nebraska Territories. But it also gave these Territories "**popular sovereignty**" on the slavery issue. This meant that residents

Abraham Lincoln, the Emancipation Proclamation, and the Thirteenth Amendment

of those territories could vote on whether or not it would be legal to own slaves there. Since both territories were north of the southern border of Missouri, this overturned the Missouri Compromise. Lincoln knew slavery might continue expanding. Later, in a brief autobiography, he wrote, "I was losing interest in politics, when the repeal of the Missouri Compromise aroused me again."

A map of the United States in 1856. Free states are in pink, slave states in gray, and US territories in green.

This map shows the United States in 1856. Free states—states that outlawed slave ownership—are in pink. States where slavery was legal are shown in gray. US territories are in green. Notice how in the middle of the map the Kansas Territory is not colored in. Due to the Kansas-Nebraska Act, it was left to its residents to determine the slavery issue. However, some proslavery and antislavery people became violent in these new territories. This series of attacks was known as **Bleeding Kansas**. Residents of Kansas drafted both proslavery and antislavery constitutions, and by 1856 the issue was not yet decided.

## Lincoln Campaigns Again

Lincoln felt it was necessary for him to speak out against the expansion of slavery, and he began traveling through Illinois, speaking for Whig candidates who opposed slavery. In 1854 he unsuccessfully ran for the US Senate as a Whig. The Whig party was splintering due to the slavery issue. Lincoln decided to join the newly formed Republican Party, which was expressly interested in ending slavery.

In 1858, he campaigned for the US Senate as a Republican. He gave one of his most famous speeches in accepting the nomination. In the "House Divided" speech, Lincoln uses a phrase from the Bible to indicate how the issue of slavery had the potential to destroy the nation.

> In my opinion, it [slavery] *will* not cease,
> until a *crisis* shall have been reached, and
> passed. "A house divided against itself cannot
> stand." I believe this government cannot
> endure, permanently half *slave* and half *free*.
> I do not expect the **Union** to be *dissolved*—I
> do not expect the house to fall—but I *do*
> expect it will cease to be divided. It will

Abraham Lincoln, the Emancipation Proclamation, and the Thirteenth Amendment

This photograph of Lincoln was taken in 1854 in Chicago when he campaigned for the US Senate as a Whig. He did not win.

become *all* one thing or *all* the other. Either the *opponents* of slavery, will arrest the further spread of it, and place it where the public mind shall rest in the belief that it is in the course of ultimate extinction; or its *advocates* will push it forward, till it shall become alike lawful in *all* the States, *old* as well as *new—North* as well as *South*.

In this speech, the "house" is the United States. It is divided against itself because it is "half *slave* and half *free*," and that division is causing violence, such as in Kansas. Lincoln says the nation can't continue that way. He paints the picture of slavery expanding not only westward but also northward into states that outlawed slavery—including Illinois. Because of the Kansas-Nebraska Act, people knew slavery had the possibility of spreading where it had been previously outlawed. In this speech, Lincoln is saying that if people wished to eliminate slavery, they must work to eliminate it *everywhere*.

## The Lincoln-Douglas Debates

Lincoln's opponent for the Illinois Senate was a familiar one: Stephen Douglas. In August of 1858, only three

A letter from Douglas to Lincoln, dated July 30, 1858. It establishes the seven Illinois cities that hosted the Lincoln-Douglas debates.

months before the election, Lincoln challenged Douglas to a series of fifty debates. At first, Douglas refused, but some newspapers called him a coward. Douglas was renowned as a debater, so he agreed to debate Lincoln in seven Illinois cities: Ottawa, Freeport, Jonesboro, Charleston, Galesburg, Quincy, and Alton. Slavery was the primary focus of the debates, especially since Douglas helped write the Kansas-Nebraska Act. The country was fascinated by these debates, and newspaper reporters were on hand to write down both speakers' remarks and telegraph them to distant cities to be published the following day.

Douglas very firmly believed only white people should have rights in our country. In the first debate at Ottawa, he said:

Abraham Lincoln, the Emancipation Proclamation, and the Thirteenth Amendment

For one, I am opposed to Negro citizenship in any and every form. I believe this Government was made on the white basis. I believe it was made by white men for the benefit of white men and their posterity for ever, and I am in favor of confining citizenship to white men, men of European birth and descent, instead of conferring it upon Negroes, Indians, and other inferior races.

At Ottawa, Lincoln attacked Douglas's idea of popular sovereignty—that people of new states could choose whether or not they allowed slave ownership. Lincoln said:

This declared indifference, but, as I must think, covert real zeal for the spread of slavery, I cannot but hate. I hate it because of the monstrous injustice of slavery itself. I hate it because it deprives our republican example of its just influence in the world— enables the enemies of free institutions, with plausibility, to taunt us as hypocrites— causes the real friends of freedom to doubt our sincerity, and especially because it forces so many really good men amongst ourselves into an open war with the very fundamental principles of civil liberty—criticizing the Declaration of Independence, and insisting that there is no right principle of action but self-interest.

Here, Lincoln explains he hates slavery because it is morally wrong to own slaves. Slavery damages the world's view of the United States as a land of liberty. How could a country that loves freedom allow one man to treat another as property? Slavery is also damaging to the slave owner. Slave owners were acting in self-interest by using slaves on their plantations, but they were also ignoring the principles of freedom stated in one of our country's most important documents. The Declaration of Independence reads: "that all men are created equal, that they are endowed by their Creator with certain unalienable Rights, that among these are Life, Liberty and the pursuit of Happiness." *All* men are equal, and have the right to be free. Lincoln believed slaves were people, not property.

However, this is not to say at this time Lincoln believed in genuine equality of people, regardless of the color of their skin. In some ways, Lincoln held racial prejudices that many people in the North did. In the fourth debate at Charleston, he talked about how the races were not equal. He did not believe slaves should be able to vote or marry white people. Lincoln said plainly that white people were superior, but that didn't mean slaves should remain slaves:

> I am not, nor ever have been, in favor of bringing about in any way the social and political equality of the white and black races, that I am not nor ever have been in favor of making voters or jurors of negroes, nor of qualifying them to hold office, nor to

The Lincoln-Douglas debates had large audiences. People even came from other states. Lincoln is at the podium. Douglas is to his left, under the flag.

intermarry with white people; and I will say in addition to this that there is a physical difference between the white and black races which I believe will forever forbid the two races living together on terms of social and political equality … I as much as any other man am in favor of having the superior position assigned to the white race. I say upon this occasion I do not perceive that because the white man is to have the superior position the Negro should be denied everything.

We know today the ideas that Lincoln describes here are wrong. However, his position allied himself with the abolitionist movement. Douglas continued to assert new states should be able to decide the slavery issue themselves. Lincoln believed slavery should be prevented from further expansion. In the end, Douglas narrowly won the election to the US Senate. Even though Lincoln didn't win the election, his campaign strengthened his political position. The debates made Lincoln famous, and they led him to become the Republican presidential nominee in 1860.

# CHAPTER TWO

# The Fight for Emancipation

American political parties were changing dramatically in the late 1850s. The changes were largely due to the Kansas-Nebraska Act, and the bloodshed in Kansas over the slavery issue. The Whigs, to which Abraham Lincoln originally belonged, no longer existed. They broke apart into proslavery and antislavery members, and the party lost its strength.

The Democratic Party, of which Stephen Douglas was a member, was also breaking apart. Not all Democrats could agree with Douglas's belief that new territories in the United States should choose whether or not to allow slavery. Some thought slaves should be treated as property, and others thought slaves were people and should not be owned.

The Republican Party was a new political party formed in Wisconsin in 1854, and it had its first statewide meeting in Michigan that year. The Republicans were very clearly against the Kansas-Nebraska Act and against slavery. Many former Whigs joined the Republicans to fight against slavery. Republicans quickly became popular across the northern United States.

## The Presidential Election of 1860

By 1860, slavery was becoming an issue that threatened to tear the United States apart. The events of Bleeding Kansas had shown fellow countrymen were willing to kill each other over the issue. The two main political parties, the Democrats and Republicans, knew it was important to choose a presidential candidate who would best shape the country they wanted. Some Southern states that allowed slavery had already begun to talk about separating from the United States if slavery were made illegal.

The Democrats tried to choose a candidate in Charleston, South Carolina, in April 1860. But some members of the party, those strongly in favor of slavery, walked out of the meeting. Eventually, the Democrats chose their candidate: Stephen Douglas. Douglas was seen as a middle-of-the-road candidate, as he neither officially approved nor disapproved of slavery. The proslavery Democrats nominated their own candidate, John Breckinridge, who was serving as vice president under US President James Buchanan.

As people in the northern United States grew to believe more strongly that slavery should be limited and eventually

This print of an American flag from the 1860 presidential election supports Lincoln. His photograph is in the upper-left corner. His first name is abbreviated "Abram."

eliminated, the Republican Party grew in power. Republicans believed every man had the right to be free and work hard, and receive the rewards of his labor. The Republicans lost the 1854 presidential election, but had won the most votes in the North, from Iowa to Maine. They realized they only needed more votes in a few more states to win the presidency.

The Republicans held their **convention**, or meeting, to choose their presidential candidate in Chicago, Illinois. Illinois was one of the states they lost to the Democrats in 1854, and also Abraham Lincoln's home state. Lincoln had impressed many people in his earlier debates with Stephen Douglas. Republicans appreciated how he opposed slavery in new territories. The Republicans chose Lincoln as their candidate. Officially, Republicans stated they would not interfere with slavery where it existed. They would seek to prevent it in any new territories or states. Some Republicans were disappointed with choosing Lincoln, though, because they wanted someone who would fight against slavery everywhere.

Abraham Lincoln, the Emancipation Proclamation, and the Thirteenth Amendment

The political cartoon below is a depiction of the presidential race as an actual footrace. Abraham Lincoln, who was 6 feet 4 inches (1.93 meters) in real life, is shown as being extremely tall. Stephen Douglas, who was 5 feet 4 inches (1.63 m) in real life, is shown as being extremely short. These drawings are known as caricatures—they are drawings of real people whose features have been exaggerated for humor.

The cartoon shows both candidates racing toward the US Capitol. The fence is difficult for Douglas because he is so short. He says, "How can I get over this Rail Fence." Lincoln's nickname was the Rail Splitter. People liked to show Lincoln's simple beginnings—he would make fences by chopping wood with an axe. It showed that Lincoln was humble, and also strong. Lincoln says the fence "can't stop

In this print, Lincoln and Douglas are racing to the US Capitol. The print implies the winner of the race would win the presidency.

me for I built it." The cartoonist believes Lincoln is the
better candidate. On the right side, a black man is trapped
in the fence, just as slaves were trapped in slavery. He says,
"You find me in dis yer Fence Massa Duglis." This crude
manner of speech is considered offensive today, but the
cartoonist is showing how slavery is literally dividing the
country, like a fence.

## Victory, with a Cost

More than 80 percent of voters participated in the 1860
presidential election, which was a huge turnout. Abraham
Lincoln received the most votes in all Northern states,
including Illinois. However, he didn't even appear on the
voting ballot in many Southern states. Republicans knew
not many people would vote for him. Still, he had enough
votes to be elected president.

His election set into motion an important series of
events. Prior to the campaign, many Southern states
threatened to **secede** from, or leave, the United States.
They believed it was right to own slaves, and that the
US government should not interfere with a state's rights
to make its own laws. They believed the North, which
was becoming more modern through industrialization,
viewed the South, which still relied heavily on farming,
as less sophisticated. Citizens of the South felt they were
not being treated as equals. The election of a Republican
president who opposed slavery confirmed their beliefs.

In December 1860, South Carolina seceded from the
Union. It wanted to be free from the US government and
all of its states. South Carolina was quickly followed by

Abraham Lincoln, the Emancipation
Proclamation, and the Thirteenth Amendment

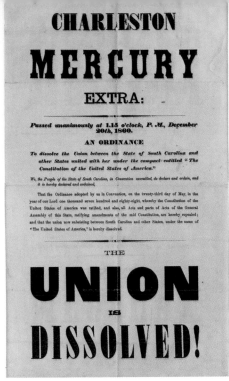

South Carolina was the first state to secede from the Union. This newspaper from Charleston, a large city in South Carolina, announces the secession.

Mississippi, Florida, Alabama, Georgia, Louisiana, and Texas. In February 1861, these states declared themselves a new country: The Confederate States of America, also known as the **Confederacy**. This was the first and only time in US history that a group of states attempted to no longer be part of the United States.

Lincoln was **inaugurated**, or officially made president of the United States, on March 4, 1861. He refused to acknowledge the existence of the new Confederacy. He believed the Confederate States were still part of the United States. Lincoln gave a speech to discuss the issues that were deeply troubling the nation. He tried to reassure the South.

In his speech, he explains how he will not violate the rights of the citizens of the South, nor of the Southern states. He also quotes a previous speech to show how his position on slavery hasn't changed. He will not attempt to make slavery illegal in places where it already exists. He said:

> Apprehension seems to exist among the
> people of the Southern States that by the
> accession of a Republican Administration their

property and their peace and personal security are to be endangered. There has never been any reasonable cause for such apprehension. Indeed, the most ample evidence to the contrary has all the while existed and been open to their inspection. It is found in nearly all the published speeches of him who now addresses you. I do but quote from one of those speeches when I declare that—

> I have no purpose, directly or indirectly, to interfere with the institution of slavery in the States where it exists. I believe I have no lawful right to do so, and I have no inclination to do so.

At the conclusion of his speech, Lincoln reminds everyone that we are all fellow citizens, and we are friends. The United States is a very special country, and we must work together to resolve our differences. He was certain people in the North and South could do so. His final words of this speech were:

> We are not enemies, but friends. We must not be enemies. Though passion may have strained, it must not break our bonds of affection. The mystic chords of memory, stretching from every battlefield and patriot grave to every living heart and hearthstone all over this broad land, will yet swell the chorus of the Union, when again touched, as surely they will be, by the better angels of our nature.

Abraham Lincoln, the Emancipation Proclamation, and the Thirteenth Amendment

# A Nation Against Itself

A civil war is a war between two or more groups of the same nation. In the American Civil War, the Northern states fought against the Southern states. In April and May of 1861, four more states joined the Confederacy: Virginia, Arkansas, Tennessee, and North Carolina. They, too, believed in their states' rights and their personal rights to own slaves. However, not all slaveholding states joined the Confederacy. Delaware, Kentucky, Maryland, and Missouri allowed slavery but did not secede. The state of West Virginia was created when part of Virginia did not wish to secede and instead joined the Union. Collectively, these five states were known as **Border States**: they were on the border between the Union and the Confederacy. They allowed slavery, but did not secede from the Union.

The Civil War was one of the worst periods in US history. It is often said that it is the bloodiest war the United States ever fought, with estimates of between six hundred thousand and seven hundred thousand people who died. The North refused to let the South become a new nation. Northerners believed the United States should be one strong country built on freedom. Southerners refused to let Northerners tell them how to run their states. Neither side was willing to compromise.

The Southern states were not convinced by Lincoln's speech. There were several attempts to get the Confederacy to rejoin the United States, also known as the Union. Every effort failed. Tensions continued to grow, and soon turned to violence.

## A Nation at War with Itself

The United States refused to surrender its property to the Confederacy. The United States would not recognize the Confederacy as a new nation. This property included military buildings. A US fort existed in Charleston, South Carolina, just off the coast on a sandbar. This was Fort Sumter. Confederate officials would not allow the Union to resupply its soldiers who lived there. The Confederacy demanded the US government surrender the fort. The United States refused. On April 12, 1861, Confederate military forces bombarded the fort for thirty-four straight hours. The fort surrendered on April 13. On April 15, Lincoln issued the call to raise seventy-five thousand volunteer troops in order to stop the rebellion of the Confederacy by force. This began the American Civil War.

Lincoln initially thought he could stop the rebellion very quickly. His call for troops said they would only serve for three months. However, the Confederacy had a series of military victories. Both sides were ready to fight and die for the causes in which they believed. Historians say the Civil War was one of the most ferocious wars ever fought by the United States.

This political cartoon shows the opinion of someone who is worried about the cost of the war to the Union. Here, Columbia (a reference to the District of Columbia, or Washington, DC) is dressed in a skirt that looks like the American flag. She says, "Mr. Lincoln, give me back my 500,000 sons!!!" The cartoonist shows he is upset with so many Union soldiers fighting in the war, especially after

Abraham Lincoln, the Emancipation Proclamation, and the Thirteenth Amendment

COLUMBIA DEMANDS HER CHILDREN!

"Columbia Demands Her Children!" is a political cartoon published in 1864. It shows that some people felt too many Union soldiers had lost their lives in the Civil War.

Lincoln first requested only 75,000. Lincoln is depicted as worried and anxious. He's scratching his head and his leg is over the back of a chair. He says, "Well the fact is—by the way that reminds me of a STORY!!!" Lincoln was known as an excellent storyteller. But here, he's trying to avoid the subject. He doesn't want to talk about the number of soldiers fighting and dying, especially when he thought the number would be much less.

## The Emancipation Proclamation

For the first year of the war, Lincoln continued to publicly insist that his only interest in fighting the Civil War was to keep the Union whole. Privately, though, he began to feel it was necessary to permanently end slavery. As the president of the United States he had no direct power to do so; slavery could only be legally abolished by Congress. However, during times of war, the president receives additional power due to being in charge of the military. Lincoln and his advisors agreed freeing slaves was included in that power.

People in the North had different opinions about freeing the slaves. Some thought that freed slaves would be able to fight as soldiers for the Union, which needed more troops. People also thought that emancipation would help destroy the South's economy. If Southern plantation owners did not have slaves to work for them, they wouldn't be able to harvest and sell their crops. Slaves also helped make supplies for the Confederate war effort. But many opponents of emancipation only cared about saving the Union. They didn't want to be in the war if it was about slavery. Some of Lincoln's advisors worried that some of the Union troops might stop fighting.

Lincoln became convinced that freeing the slaves was the correct moral action as well as a wise military move. He issued a first draft of the Emancipation Proclamation in September of 1862. He gave the Confederacy one hundred days to return to the Union. If the rebel states refused, their slaves would be freed. No states returned. On January 1, 1863, the Emancipation Proclamation was enacted as a war measure by the president in his role as Commander-in-Chief of the United States military. It reads:

> I do order and declare that all persons held as slaves within said designated States, and parts of States, are, and henceforward shall be free; and that the Executive government of the United States, including the military and naval authorities thereof, will recognize and maintain the freedom of said persons.

Abraham Lincoln, the Emancipation Proclamation, and the Thirteenth Amendment

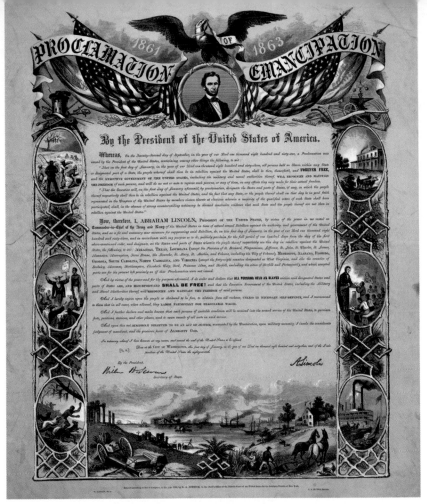

An illustrated version of the Emancipation Proclamation. The pictures on the left show the difficult lives of slaves. The pictures on the right show a new, prosperous nation where slaves are now free.

And I hereby enjoin upon the people so declared to be free to abstain from all violence, unless in necessary self-defence; and I recommend to them that, in all cases when allowed, they labor faithfully for reasonable wages.

And I further declare and make known, that such persons of suitable condition, will

be received into the armed service of the
United States to garrison forts, positions,
stations, and other places, and to man vessels
of all sorts in said service.

By issuing this proclamation, Lincoln freed all slaves
under Confederate control. He encourages the newly
freed slaves to be peaceful, and to be paid for their work.
He also allows former slaves to serve in the Union army
to help defeat the Confederacy.

The illustrated version of the Proclamation of
Emancipation from 1864 (see previous page) depicts many
of the values for which it stands. It shows the strength
of the Union with its flags and eagle at the top. The
pictures on the left show the negative aspects of slavery:
a master with a whip, a slave auction, and an escaping
slave being attacked by dogs. The picture on the bottom
shows the illustrator's hope for the future; on the left are
the remnants of war. They emerge on the right as a picture
of a whole and prosperous nation. The three pictures on
the right show a healthy plantation with no slaves, black
children getting an education, and successful commerce
under the American flag. Abraham Lincoln, the author,
receives prominent focus in the circle centered at the top.

By issuing the Emancipation Proclamation, Lincoln
knew he was making a decision that would change
US history. Some reactions were immediate, and some
continue to be felt to this day. Upon signing it, he said,
"If my name ever goes into history it will be for this act,
and my whole soul is in it."

Abraham Lincoln, the Emancipation
Proclamation, and the Thirteenth Amendment

# The Reaction to the Emancipation Proclamation and the Thirteenth Amendment

The Emancipation Proclamation changed US history, but the Civil War still raged on. The Confederacy would not accept emancipation as law. It would take almost three more years until *all* slaves in the United States were free.

## Immediate Reactions

Many Northerners, particularly Republicans, were thrilled by Lincoln's signing of the Emancipation Proclamation into law. They believed the United States could not be a free country unless all its citizens were free. Some Democrats, though, only wanted peace. They wanted the Union and the Confederacy to agree to stop the war. They felt that emancipation only made the problem worse. Certainly, the Southern states hated the Emancipation Proclamation. They were fighting to keep slavery legal.

Black Americans were joyous upon the news of the abolition of slavery. They could no longer be legally forced to work for someone else under inhumane conditions. Frederick Douglass was a famous black **orator**, or speaker, who gave many antislavery speeches across the North. About a month after Lincoln freed the slaves, Douglass spoke at a school in New York City. He said:

> I congratulate you, upon what may be called the greatest event of our nation's history, if not the greatest event of the century. … Color is no longer a crime or a badge of bondage. At last the out-spread wings of the American Eagle afford shelter and protection to men of all colors, all countries and climes, and the long oppressed black man may honorably fall or gloriously flourish under the star-spangled banner. I stand here tonight not only as a colored man and an American, but by the express decision of the Attorney-General of the United States, as a colored citizen, having, in common with all other citizens, a stake in the safety, prosperity, honor, and glory of a common country. We are all liberated by this proclamation.

Abraham Lincoln, the Emancipation Proclamation, and the Thirteenth Amendment

Frederick Douglass was an impassioned speaker for the rights of black people. He wrote several autobiographies and created newspapers that promoted equality.

Douglass explains the power of the Emancipation Proclamation. He describes how the color of a person's skin no longer identifies him or her as a slave. He says that America is now a place where people of all skin colors are protected, and they are all given freedom. This makes the newly freed slaves true citizens of the United States and that white and black people together have a common interest in making sure the country succeeds in its vision of liberty.

Newly freed slaves were able to help the Union more directly, too. As Lincoln and his advisors predicted, many of the former slaves signed up to serve in the Union army to help defeat the Confederacy. In May 1863, the US War Department established the United States Colored Troops to help recruit black soldiers. By the end of the war, more than 180,000 black men had enlisted in the Union military. One out of every eight men serving in the war was black.

The photograph on page 34, taken after the Emancipation Proclamation, shows Company E of the 4th Colored US Infantry in Washington, DC. Notice how distinguished the men look in their formal military attire. The soldiers are demonstrating their pride and also their strength by showing their guns. The man on the left

Company E of the 4th Colored US Infantry. This photograph was taken at Fort Lincoln in Washington, DC. About 180,000 black troops fought for the Union.

has a sword. He is an **officer,** or a leader of the troops. This sword could be used for fighting, be also was used to direct troops in battle. This photograph shows proud and powerful black men, and is very different from the idea of a black person who is a slave and piece of property.

Some people, though, didn't think the Emancipation Proclamation did much good. It only freed slaves on land controlled by the Confederacy. That meant a US law had no real impact. There were several states that remained loyal to the Union but that allowed slavery. Those slaves were not immediately set free. Still, people realized this was a major change. It encouraged slaves in the South to escape their owners. Slowly, as Lincoln hoped, the South lost the workers who helped supply its armies.

Abraham Lincoln, the Emancipation
Proclamation, and the Thirteenth Amendment

## Remembering Those Who Died for the Cause

The Civil War continued on. The Union was making slow but steady advances into Confederate territory. In early July, both sides fought in Gettysburg, Pennsylvania. The Battle of Gettysburg would become the deadliest battle of the war, with over 45,000 soldiers killed. Some people also marked it as a turning point. The Confederacy had some military successes up until this battle. However, at Gettysburg, the Union forced the Confederacy to retreat, and the battle was considered to be a great Union victory.

On November 19, 1863, Abraham Lincoln gave a speech at this battlefield. The occasion was to establish a national cemetery for the Union soldiers who lost their lives there. Lincoln delivered the Gettysburg Address, which has become one of the most famous speeches in American history. It is also very short: it took Lincoln about two minutes to deliver it. He said:

> But, in a larger sense, we cannot dedicate, we can not consecrate, we can not hallow this ground. The brave men, living and dead, who struggled here, have consecrated it, far above our poor power to add or detract. The world will little note, nor long remember what we say here, but it can never forget what they did here. It is for us the living, rather, to be dedicated here to the unfinished work which they who fought here have thus far so nobly advanced. It is rather for us to be here dedicated to the great task remaining

before us—that from these honored dead we take increased devotion to that cause for which they gave the last full measure of devotion—that we here highly resolve that these dead shall not have died in vain—that this nation, under God, shall have a new birth of freedom—and that government of the people, by the people, for the people, shall not perish from the earth.

Lincoln at Gettysburg. Lincoln is in the middle of the photo, not wearing a hat, facing the crowd. He is to the left of the tall, bearded man in the center.

Lincoln says no living person can make this battlefield more important through a speech. The soldiers who died have made the land important. They gave the ultimate sacrifice. They gave their lives. Furthermore, he says those who are still living have an important obligation. The survivors have the obligation to finish and win the war for which the soldiers died. Lincoln says we must work for "a new birth of freedom." That new freedom began with the

Abraham Lincoln, the Emancipation Proclamation, and the Thirteenth Amendment

Emancipation Proclamation. If the Union did not win the war, it would not secure freedom for everyone, and the soldiers would have died "in vain," or, for no reason.

## The End of the Civil War

In 1863 and 1864, Union forces drove deeper into Confederate territory. Lincoln ran for reelection for president in 1864, against a major general for the Union Army, George McClellan. Lincoln was determined to win the war. McClellan ran as a Democrat. The Democrats believed peace was most important and a settlement should be reached with the Confederacy. Personally, McClellan did not believe this, and it angered some Democrats.

The political cartoon below favors McClellan. He is in the middle, saying, "The Union must be preserved

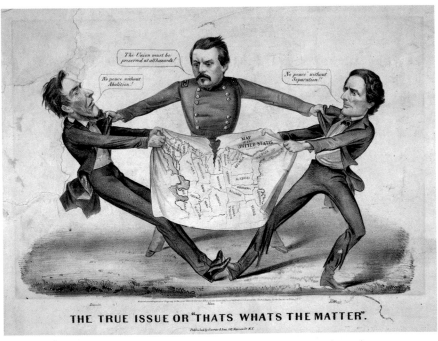

This cartoon from the 1864 presidential election shows Lincoln and Jefferson Davis literally tearing the United States apart.

at all hazards!" On the left, Abraham Lincoln says, "No peace without Abolition," a reference to how he refused to negotiate with the Confederacy unless they would give up slavery. On the right, Jefferson Davis, president of the Confederacy, says, "No peace without Separation!!" The South would not stop fighting until it left the Union permanently. The cartoon shows Lincoln and Davis willing to rip the United States (shown as a map) apart, while McClellan is a reasonable figure of authority trying to stop both of them.

As 1864 went on, the Union had several key military victories. One of the most notable was the capture of Atlanta, an important Southern city. Soldiers liked Lincoln. They voted for him, and told their friends to vote for him, too. Lincoln won reelection by more four hundred thousand votes.

By the time he gave his second inaugural speech, the war was almost over. The Union had destroyed most of the Confederate forces. He knew that the nation would need healing. He proposed doing so kindly in order to have "lasting peace." All of the nation's citizens needed to be forgiving of each other. He said:

> With malice toward none, with charity
> for all, with firmness in the right as God
> gives us to see the right, let us strive on to
> finish the work we are in, to bind up the
> nation's wounds, to care for him who shall
> have borne the battle and for his widow
> and his orphan, to do all which may achieve

Abraham Lincoln, the Emancipation
Proclamation, and the Thirteenth Amendment

# The Assassination of Lincoln

Lincoln was **assassinated**, or killed, by John Wilkes Booth. Booth was a well-known actor and performed in plays in Washington, DC. He strongly hated Lincoln for ending slavery and defeating the Confederacy. Before killing the president, Booth had originally planned to kidnap him to make demands. That plan failed. After hearing Lincoln give a speech where he supported freeing all slaves, Booth made up his mind. He was going to murder the president.

On the morning of April 14, 1865, Booth learned that the Lincolns would be attending a play later that night. The play, *Our American Cousin*, was presented at Ford's Theatre in Washington. Booth frequently worked there, and therefore was allowed access to the entire space. The Lincolns sat on a private balcony in the theater. While the play was going on, Booth slipped behind them and shot the president. He shouted, "*Sic semper tyrannis!*"—"Thus always to tyrants!" He then jumped onto the stage, breaking his leg. He escaped, but was tracked down and shot on April 26. Lincoln was the first US president to be assassinated.

and cherish a just and lasting peace among ourselves and with all nations.

The Civil War ended when the Confederacy surrendered to the Union at Appomattox Court House, Virginia, on April 9, 1865. The Union had prevailed, and the Southern states returned to the United States.

The Confederacy surrendered to the Union in this house in Appomattox Court House, Virginia. The house was owned by Wilmer McLean. The McLean family sits on the steps.

Unfortunately, Lincoln didn't have long to enjoy the victory. On April 14, he was shot by a man who still believed in the Confederacy, and he died the following day.

## The Thirteenth Amendment

Before the end of the war and Lincoln's death, the United States was in the process of making a law that would abolish slavery everywhere. This law was so important that it would amend, or change, the US Constitution. The Constitution provides the most important laws and freedoms of the United States.

Since the Constitution is so important, the process to change it is long and difficult. Lincoln was worried

A cover illustration from *Harper's Weekly*, an important political magazine, shows the House of Representatives passing the Thirteenth Amendment.

that courts might later find the Emancipation Proclamation illegal since he issued it under his special war powers. He knew the United States needed a permanent change that couldn't be questioned.

The US Senate voted in favor of an **amendment** abolishing slavery in April 1864. The House of Representatives did not. Both the Senate and the House need to agree to an amendment. After Lincoln won his reelection, he pushed for the House to vote again. They voted in favor of the amendment on January 31, 1865, and Lincoln approved and signed it the next day. The Thirteenth Amendment is very short:

> Section 1. Neither slavery nor involuntary servitude, except as a punishment for crime whereof the party shall have been duly convicted, shall exist within the United States, or any place subject to their jurisdiction.
>
> Section 2. Congress shall have power to enforce this article by appropriate legislation.

It reads that slavery cannot exist anywhere in the United States. Only prisoners could be made to work without being paid. The amendment also gave Congress the power to pass more laws to make sure the amendment was being upheld.

The amendment then needed to be ratified, or approved, by two-thirds of the states. Lincoln's home state of Illinois was the first to approve it, on the same day he did. The final four states to reach the necessary number were from the former Confederacy. On December 18, 1865, the Thirteenth Amendment became part of the Constitution. Although the nation was still shocked and saddened by Lincoln's death, the abolitionists had won. Slavery was permanently outlawed in the United States.

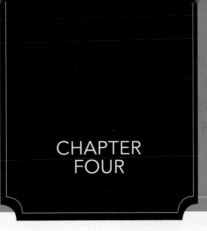

# Lincoln's Legacy

Abraham Lincoln changed racial equality through the Emancipation Proclamation. Emancipation then became permanent law in the Thirteenth Amendment. But Americans needed to do more to ensure people of all races were equals.

Although the Civil War had ended, the nation needed to heal and rebuild. Many farms, towns, and cities were destroyed due to the fighting. The process of repairing the United States physically, socially, and legally after the Civil War was known as **Reconstruction**.

## The Fourteenth and Fifteenth Amendments

During Reconstruction, people held different opinions about the roles newly freed slaves should have in society.

Andrew Johnson was sworn in as the seventeenth president of the United States on April 15, 1865, a few hours after Lincoln died.

Some thought they should immediately be treated as equals. Some Northerners held racist beliefs that blacks were not equal to whites. And in the South, many people still believed blacks could only be slaves.

Andrew Johnson became the US president after Lincoln was killed. He believed the Confederate states should be brought back into the United States as quickly as possible. But some Republicans didn't think that would guarantee true freedom for the former slaves. They proposed two additional amendments to the Constitution.

The Fourteenth Amendment was adopted in 1868 despite strong protests from Southern states. The first, and most important, section reads:

> All persons born or naturalized in the United States, and subject to the jurisdiction thereof, are citizens of the United States and of the State wherein they reside. No State shall make or enforce any law which shall abridge the privileges or immunities of citizens of the United States; nor shall any State deprive any person of life, liberty,

Abraham Lincoln, the Emancipation Proclamation, and the Thirteenth Amendment

or property, without due process of law; nor deny to any person within its jurisdiction the equal protection of the laws.

This amendment grants citizenship to *all* people born in the United States, regardless of color. It also confirms citizenship for immigrants who choose to become US citizens. The amendment says no state can restrict the rights and privileges of any citizen. States must treat citizens equally in terms of the law.

Some people did not believe the Fourteenth Amendments guaranteed black Americans' right to vote. Congress proposed an additional amendment to address this issue. Again there was strong protest from Southern states. But the Fifteenth Amendment was ratified and became law in 1870. Like the Thirteenth Amendment, it is very short:

The right of citizens of the United States to vote shall not be denied or abridged by the United States or by any State on account of race, color, or previous condition of servitude.

This amendment is straightforward. No state in the United States can deny a citizen the right to vote based on skin color, or whether or not he used to be a slave. In the five years after Lincoln's death, former slaves were permanently freed, given the same rights as white citizens, and specifically given the right to vote. The work he began with the Emancipation Proclamation now had permanent legal authority.

*The Result of the Fifteenth Amendment* shows scenes of freed black Americans. The Fifteenth Amendment gave US citizens of all races the right to vote. Lincoln's portrait is in the upper left.

## Frederick Douglass on Lincoln

In April 1876, a statue showing Abraham Lincoln emancipating a slave was dedicated in Washington, DC. Frederick Douglass gave a speech about what Lincoln meant to the emancipation movement. Douglass's descriptions aren't entirely positive. Earlier in his political career, Lincoln publicly stated that white people were superior to black people. Prior to the Civil War, Lincoln said he would not outlaw slavery, but only wanted to prevent it from expanding. And during the early days of the Civil War, Lincoln said his goal was to restore the Union, not abolish slavery.

In his speech, Douglass describes how he felt Lincoln favored whites:

Abraham Lincoln, the Emancipation Proclamation, and the Thirteenth Amendment

> He was preeminently the white man's President, entirely devoted to the welfare of white men. He was ready and willing at any time during the first years of his administration to deny, postpone, and sacrifice the rights of humanity in the colored people to promote the welfare of the white people of this country.

Some might view this as a harsh view of Lincoln. But it does point out the reality of Lincoln's public beliefs. However, Douglass states Lincoln's personal feelings about slavery later in the speech: "Though Mr. Lincoln shared the prejudices of his white fellow-countrymen against the Negro, it is hardly necessary to say that in his heart of hearts he loathed and hated slavery."

Douglass also describes the importance of the Emancipation Proclamation:

> Can any colored man, or any white man friendly to the freedom of all men, ever forget the night which followed the first day of January, 1863, when the world was to see if Abraham Lincoln would prove to be as good as his word? I shall never forget that memorable night, when in a distant city I waited and watched at a public meeting, with three thousand others not less anxious than myself, for the word of deliverance which we have heard read today. Nor shall I ever forget the outburst of joy and thanksgiving that

rent the air when the lightning brought to us the emancipation proclamation.

Douglass shows how much hope and joy the Proclamation brought to black people, and that Lincoln was a good man for issuing it. By the end of his speech, Douglass celebrates Abraham Lincoln. He knew a president has many important decisions to make, and Lincoln had to make those decisions carefully. Those decisions led to freeing the slaves.

## Segregation and Jim Crow Laws

Black Americans were given the same rights as their fellow white citizens. However, many people still did not believe former slaves should be treated equally.

In the South, state governments passed new laws that limited black participation in voting. Some states required **poll taxes**. A poll tax requires someone to pay to vote. As many of the former slaves were poor, they couldn't afford to vote. Other states required literacy tests to vote. Many slaves were not educated and therefore could not read. When they became free, they were denied the right to vote because they were illiterate.

People also became violent when faced with the new rights of former slaves. People who held the beliefs that whites were superior to blacks formed groups. They would intimidate black people to prevent them from voting. They would also physically threaten and attack people, and sometimes murdered their victims.

Some whites thought blacks should not use the same schools, railroad cars, and even drinking fountains as

Abraham Lincoln, the Emancipation
Proclamation, and the Thirteenth Amendment

# Who Was Jim Crow?

The name "Jim Crow" came from a character portrayed by an actor in a minstrel show. A minstrel show was a live show of comedy and music. They were very popular in the 1800s. Often, white actors performed in blackface. Blackface is when a white actor paints his face to look like a black man. Today, this is considered highly offensive.

These shows often depicted black people as unintelligent and lazy. They also showed black people as having musical talent, and included songs such as slave spirituals.

At the time, people had mixed feelings about minstrel shows. They were clearly racist, and portrayed black people as stereotypes rather than real people. However, for some white people, the shows were their only opportunity to experience the lives of black people, and it made them more aware of issues such as slavery. The overall portrayal was negative, though, and "Jim Crow" became a way to describe laws that treated black people as different—and worse—than whites.

whites did. In 1896, the Supreme Court agreed with them. In the case *Plessy v. Ferguson*, the Supreme Court said it was legal for different races to have different facilities as long as they were "separate but equal." For example, there could be two schools, one for whites, and one for blacks, as long as they were of the same quality.

This legalized racial **segregation**, where people of different skin colors are kept separate. In reality, the facilities were rarely equal for blacks. For example, a white library might be able to buy new books, while a black

A small, colored-only school in Anthoston, Kentucky, in 1916. Seperate schools for different races were legal due to the *Plessy v. Ferguson* court decision.

library in the same city would receive less funding and have to rely more on used and older books. There were laws that segregated schools, public transportation, rest rooms, and restaurants. These were known as **Jim Crow laws**, and they were enforced well into the twentieth century.

## The Civil Rights Movement

In the 1950s and 1960s, people knew the work begun by Lincoln was unfinished. It was clear that "separate but equal" was not effective, especially when black facilities weren't equal. This led to the Civil Rights Movement. People of all races worked together for the rights of everyone. Those involved fought against Jim Crow laws and other inequalities.

A famous leader of this movement was Martin Luther King Jr. Although some whites were still violently attacking and killing blacks due to their race, King

Abraham Lincoln, the Emancipation
Proclamation, and the Thirteenth Amendment

believed racial problems should be solved nonviolently. He helped organize protests, boycotts, and marches to promote equality.

In 1963, one hundred years after the Emancipation Proclamation, King delivered his famous speech: "I Have a Dream." After leading a march in Washington, DC, he spoke to a crowd of more than 250,000 people from the steps of the Lincoln Memorial.

King begins with a reference to Lincoln's Gettysburg Address (which begins, "Four score and seven years ago"), and talks about the Emancipation Proclamation:

> Five score years ago, a great American, in whose symbolic shadow we stand today, signed the Emancipation Proclamation. This momentous decree came as a great beacon light of hope to millions of Negro slaves who had been seared in the flames of withering injustice. It came as a joyous daybreak to end the long night of their captivity.
>
> But one hundred years later, the Negro still is not free. One hundred years later, the life of the Negro is still sadly crippled by the manacles of segregation and the chains of discrimination.

King describes how important Lincoln's proclamation was. Like Frederick Douglass, King describes the hope and joy of eliminating slavery. King also points out that even though a hundred years had passed, black people still were not truly free. Their lives were trapped by discrimination.

Martin Luther King Jr. at the Lincoln Memorial. He delivered his famous "I Have a Dream" speech on August 28, 1963, to a huge audience.

Later, King uses the title of his speech:

> I have a dream that one day this nation will rise up and live out the true meaning of its creed: "We hold these truths to be self-evident, that all men are created equal."
>
> I have a dream that one day on the red hills of Georgia, the sons of former slaves and the sons of former slave owners will be able to sit down together at the table of brotherhood …
>
> I have a dream that my four little children will one day live in a nation where they will not be judged by the color of their skin but by the content of their character.

King is hopeful that America can truly be a place where everyone is equal. He wants all Americans to judge

Abraham Lincoln, the Emancipation Proclamation, and the Thirteenth Amendment

a person based on character, not skin color. King's speech was very powerful and inspired many people to share his vision of equality. Tragically, similar to Lincoln, King was later murdered for his beliefs.

Through the work of King and other leaders, many laws were passed for equal rights. These laws helped prevent racial discrimination in voting, employment, housing, and other areas of daily life.

## Lincoln's Legacy

More than 150 years ago, Abraham Lincoln began the work of ensuring equality for all US citizens by issuing the Emancipation Proclamation. Since then, many people have built on his good work, often facing threats, violence, and unjust laws. Some people still believe in racial discrimination, and the fight for total equality is not finished.

Lincoln successfully steered the United States through an incredibly difficult and bloody war. He also began one of the most fundamental social changes in the United States. Historians and the public often rate Lincoln as the best US president.

Abraham Lincoln was a great president. He was a great man. He was the Great Emancipator.

This photograph of Lincoln was taken in February 1865, only two months before he was assassinated by John Wilkes Booth.

# Chronology

**Dates** in green pertain to events discussed in this volume.

**1619** The African slave trade begins in North America.

**1789** US Constitution goes into effect.

**1777–1804** Slavery is abolished in the northern states.

**1808** The foreign slave trade is abolished by Great Britain and the US.

**1809** Abraham Lincoln born on February 12 in Hodgenville, Kentucky

**1830** The Lincoln family moves to Illinois.

**1832** Abraham Lincoln loses an election to serve in the Illinois state legislature.

**1833** The American Anti-Slavery Society is founded in Philadelphia.

**1834** Abraham Lincoln is elected to the Illinois House of Representatives.

**1837–1839** The Grimké sisters speak against slavery to overflow audiences in New York and New England.

**1849** Harriet Tubman escapes from slavery into Pennsylvania.

**1850** US Congress passes the Fugitive Slave Act.

**1851** *Uncle Tom's Cabin* runs as a serial in the abolitionist newspaper *National Era* in Washington, DC.

**1852** Stowe's complete novel, *Uncle Tom's Cabin*, sells millions of copies.

**1854** Congress approves the Kansas-Nebraska Act; Abraham Lincoln loses an election to serve as a US senator.

**1855–1860** Harriet Tubman rescues freedom seekers and leads them from Maryland to Canada.

**1856** Proslavery activists attack the antislavery town of Lawrence, Kansas; John Brown leads a raid on a proslavery family, which launches a three-month conflict known as "Bleeding Kansas."

**1857** Supreme Court hands down decision in the *Dred Scott v. Sanford* case.

**1859** John Brown launches an attack at Harpers Ferry.

**1860** Abraham Lincoln is elected president; South Carolina secedes from the Union.

**1861** Abraham Lincoln is inaugurated as the sixteenth president of the United States; Civil War begins.

**1863** Lincoln's Emancipation Proclamation frees the slaves in Confederate-held territory; Lincoln delivers the Gettysburg Address.

**1864** Abraham Lincoln is elected to a second term as US president.

**1865** The Civil War ends; the Thirteenth Amendment to the US Constitution abolishes slavery; President Lincoln is assassinated.

**1866** The American Equal Rights Association is formed. Its goals are to establish equal rights and the vote for women and African Americans.

**1868** Fourteenth Amendment grants US citizenship to former slaves.

**1870** Fifteenth Amendment gives black men the right to vote.

**1896** A group of black civil rights activists, form the National Association of Colored Women in Washington, DC. The group works to further civil rights for blacks and obtain the vote for women.

**1963** Martin Luther King delivers "I Have a Dream" on the steps of the Lincoln Memorial one hundred years after the Emancipation Proclamation.

# Glossary

**abolitionist**  A person who wanted to end slavery.

**amendment**  An official change to the US Constitution.

**assassinate**  To murder an important or famous person.

**Bleeding Kansas**  A series of violent fights between proslavery and antislavery forces in the Kansas Territory.

**Border States**  States that remained loyal to the Union during the Civil War but allowed slavery: Delaware, Kentucky, Maryland, Missouri, and West Virginia.

**cash crop**  Plants grown on a farm to sell for money, as opposed to plants grown for food.

**Confederacy**  The group of states that seceded from the US in the Civil War. Also known as the Confederate States of America or the South.

**convention**  A meeting of a political party to choose their candidates to run for elections.

**emancipation**  Making slaves free.

**inaugurate**  To officially put someone into an elected position.

**Jim Crow laws** Laws that allowed for segregation and discrimination of black Americans.

**officer** A person who is a leader in the military.

**orator** A person who gives speeches.

**plantation** A large farm.

**poll tax** A fee charged to vote in an election.

**popular sovereignty** The belief promoted by Stephen Douglas that US territories should vote for themselves whether or not they would allow slavery.

**ratify** To formally approve and adopt an amendment to the Constitution.

**Reconstruction** The time period immediately following the Civil War to repair the US legally, socially, and physically.

**secede** To officially leave.

**segregation** The separation of people based on skin color.

**Union** The United States, particularly those states that remained loyal to the nation in the Civil War. Also known as the North.

# Further Information

## Books

Fleming, Candace. *The Lincolns: A Scrapbook Look at Abraham and Mary*. New York: Schwartz and Wade Books, 2008.

Freedman, Russell. *Lincoln: A Photobiography*. New York: Clarion Books, 1987.

Holzer, Harold, and Joshua Wolf Shenk, eds. *In Lincoln's Hand: His Original Manuscripts*. New York: Bantam Books, 2009.

Howell, Maria, ed. *The Emancipation Proclamation*. Farmington Hills, MI: Thomson Gale, 2006.

Meltzer, Milton, ed. *Lincoln in His Own Words*. San Diego, CA: Harcourt Brace and Company, 1993.

## Websites

**Abraham Lincoln Presidential Library Foundation**

www.underhishat.org

"Under His Hat" offers digital versions of primary sources from the Lincoln Collection in Springfield, Illinois. The website includes documents and photographs of items used by Lincoln.

**Library of Congress**

www.loc.gov/exhibits/lincoln

In "With Malice Toward None: The Abraham Lincoln Bicentennial Exhibition," the Library of Congress displays a vast archive of material related to Abraham Lincoln. Many key primary sources are chosen for display, with each one thoroughly explained.

**National Archives and Records Administration**

www.archives.gov/exhibits/featured_documents/emancipation_proclamation

All five pages of The Emancipation Proclamation, as signed by President Lincoln, are digitized here in sharp detail. There are descriptions of the physical document and the importance of the laws it enacted.

# Bibliography

Abraham Lincoln Historical Digitization Project. "The Lincoln/Douglas Debates of 1858." Accessed December 19, 2014. http://lincoln.lib.niu.edu/ lincolndouglas/index.html.

———. "Lincoln/Net." Accessed December 19, 2014. http://lincoln.lib.niu.edu.

Blackpast.org. "Douglass, Frederick, 1817–1895." Accessed January 23, 2015. http://www.blackpast.org/ aah/douglass-frederick-1817-1895.

Burgan, Michael. *The Lincoln-Douglas Debates*. Minneapolis, MN: Compass Point Books, 2006.

Carey, Jr., Charles. *The Emancipation Proclamation*. Mankato, MN: The Child's World, 2009.

Civil War Trust. "Civil War Primary Sources." Accessed January 23, 2015. www.civilwar.org/education/history/ primarysources.

Gates, Henry Louis Jr., ed. *Lincoln on Race and Slavery*. Princeton, NJ: Princeton University Press, 2009.

House Divided Project. "Emancipation 101." Accessed December 19, 2014. housedivided.dickinson.edu/sites/ emancipation.

January, Brendan. *Cornerstones of Freedom: The Lincoln-Douglas Debates*. New York: Children's Press, 1998.

———. *Cornerstones of Freedom: The Emancipation Proclamation*. New York: Children's Press, 1998.

Jim Crow Museum. "The Origins of Jim Crow." Accessed January 30, 2015. www.ferris.edu/HTMLS/news/jimcrow/origins.htm.

Library of Congress. "13th Amendment to the U.S. Constitution." Accessed January 23, 2015. www.loc.gov/rr/program/bib/ourdocs/13thamendment.html.

————. "The African-American Mosaic: Abolition." Accessed December 20, 2014. www.loc.gov/exhibits/african/afam005.html.

————. "African-American Odyssey." Accessed December 23, 2014. memory.loc.gov/ammem/aaohtml/exhibit/aointro.html.

Marrin, Albert. *Commander in Chief: Abraham Lincoln and the Civil War.* New York: Dutton Children's Books, 1997.

Martin Luther King, Jr. Research and Education Institute. "'I Have a Dream,' Address at March on Washington for Jobs and Freedom." Accessed January 30, 2014. http://mlk-kpp01.stanford.edu/index.php/encyclopedia/documentsentry/doc_august_28_1963_i_have_a_dream.

Miller Center. "American President: Abraham Lincoln (1809–1865)." Accessed December 19, 2014. millercenter.org/president/lincoln.

Public Broadcasting Service. "The Civil War: The War." Accessed January 23, 2015. www.pbs.org/civilwar/war.

Sandler, Martin W. *Lincoln through the Lens.* New York: Walker and Company, 2008.

Tackach, James. *The Emancipation Proclamation: Abolishing Slavery in the South.* San Diego, CA: Lucent Books, 1999.

# Index

Abraham Lincoln, the Emancipation Proclamation, and the Thirteenth Amendment

King, Martin Luther, Jr.,
  50–53, **52**

Lincoln, Abraham, **8, 13,**
  **21, 53**
  death, 39
  elected President, 22–23
  Gettysburg Address,
    35–36, **36,** 51
  "House Divided"
    speech, 12–13
  political party, 8, 12,
    17, 20, 22
  Lincoln-Douglas debates,
    13–17, **17**

McClellan, George,
  37–38, **37**
Missouri Compromise,
  10–11

**officer,** 34
**orator,** 32

**plantation,** 5, 10, 16, 28,
  30
*Plessy v. Ferguson,* 49–50
political cartoons, 21–22,
  26–27, 37–38

political parties,
    *See* Democratic;
      Republican; Whig
**poll tax,** 48
**popular sovereignty,** 10, 15

**ratify,** 42
**Reconstruction,** 43
Republican party, 12, 17,
  19–20, 22, 31, 44

**scccde,** 22–23, 25
**segregation,** 49, 51
slaves, 4–6, **5,** 10–11, 16,
  18, 22, 25, 27–28, 30–34,
  39, 43–45, 48, 51–52

**Union,** 12, 22–28, 30,
  32–35, 37–40, 46
United States
  Constitution, 40, 42, 44
  Fifteenth Amendment,
    43, 45–46
  Fourteenth
    Amendment, 43–45
  Thirteenth Amendment,
    40–43

Whig party, 8, 12, 18–19

## About the Author

**B. J. BEST** was born and lives in Wisconsin, the birthplace of the Republican Party. He has also lived in Freeport, Illinois, the site of the second of the famous debates between Stephen Douglas and Abraham Lincoln. He teaches writing at Carroll University. Although laws and beliefs can be slow to change, he is proud to live in a country that continually fights for the equal rights and treatment of all of its citizens.

Abraham Lincoln, the Emancipation
Proclamation, and the Thirteenth Amendment